easy meals

Fish & Seafood

p

This is a Parragon Book
First printed in 2001

Parragon
Queen Street House
4 Queen Street
Bath BA1 1HE
United Kingdom

ISBN: 0-75255-335-6

Printed in Spain

Produced by The Bridgewater Book Company Ltd, Lewes, East Sussex

Creative Director Terry Jeavons
Art Director Sarah Howerd
Editorial Director Fiona Biggs
Senior Editor Mark Truman
Editorial Assistant Tom Kitch
Page Make-up Chris Akroyd

NOTES FOR THE READER

- This book uses both metric and imperial measurements. Follow the same units of measurement throughout; do not mix metric and imperial.
- All spoon measurements are level: teaspoons are assumed to be 5 ml, and tablespoons are assumed to be 15 ml.
- Unless otherwise stated, milk is assumed to be full-fat, eggs and individual vegetables such as potatoes are medium-sized, and pepper is freshly ground black pepper.
- Recipes using raw or very lightly cooked eggs should be avoided by infants, the elderly, pregnant women, convalescents, and anyone suffering from an illness.
- Optional ingredients, variations, and serving suggestions have not been included in the calculations.
- The times given are an approximate guide only. Preparation times differ according to the techniques used by different people and the cooking times vary as a result of the type of oven used.

Contents

Introduction

When it comes to choosing ingredients for a meal that's easy to prepare and cook, there is nothing better than fish or seafood. It's full of protein and minerals, low in fat, comes in a whole variety of shapes, textures, and even colours, and cooks very quickly – indeed, over-cooking fish does it no favours at all. Best of all, it is incredibly versatile, working well in all kinds of dishes, including soups, patés, and salads, in rice or pasta dishes, or simply grilled or baked in the oven.

Fish makes an excellent partner for flavours such as garlic, chillies, herbs and citrus fruits; for vegetables, cheese and eggs; and even for meat in dishes such as jambalaya. It can form the basis of a quick mid-week supper – canned tuna must be one of the most popular store-cupboard essentials, usually loved by both adults and children – or an elegant dinner party, perhaps using the more unusual swordfish, red snapper, John Dory, sea bass or scallops.

guide to recipe key	
easy	Recipes are graded as follows: 1 pea = easy; 2 peas = very easy; 3 peas = extremely easy.
serves 4	Most of the recipes in this book serve four people. Simply halve the ingredients to serve two, taking care not to mix imperial and metric measurements.
15 minutes	Preparation time. Where recipes include marinating, soaking, standing, or chilling, times for these are listed separately: eg, 15 minutes, plus 30 minutes to marinate.
15 minutes	Cooking time. Cooking times do not include the cooking of rice or noodles served with the main dishes.

Fish and seafood form a key part of the diet in many countries, so the dishes included here are gathered from around the world – Mexico, Thailand (where far more fish is consumed than meat), China, the Mediterranean and the Caribbean. They are a combination of familiar and well-loved classic dishes – including Smoked Mackerel Paté, Chinese Fried Rice and Cod Italienne – and some exciting new ideas – Thai Fish Cakes with Hot Peanut Dip, Crab Risotto with Roasted Peppers, and Baked Fish with Pepper, Chillies & Basil, to name just a few.

Gourmets and the health-conscious are delighted to be served a fish dish – so choose your recipe and get ready to impress!

Moules Marinara, page 64

Soups
& Starters

Fish makes a wonderful light starter to a meal, and is ideal if it is to be followed by a more substantial meat dish. The recipes in this section are also fun if your meal has a regional theme – why not try serving Mexican Fish & Roasted Tomato Soup as part of a Mexican feast, or home-made Taramasalata with Pita wedges if you want to conjure up happy memories of hot, sunny days in the Mediterranean.

Mexican Fish & Roasted Tomato Soup

INGREDIENTS

5 ripe tomatoes

5 garlic cloves,
    unpeeled

500 g/1 lb 2 oz snapper,
    cut into chunks

1 litre/1¾ pints fish
    stock, or water plus a
    fish stock cube or two

2–3 tbsp olive oil

1 onion, chopped

2 fresh green chillies,
    such as serrano,
    deseeded and thinly
    sliced

lime wedges, to serve

❶ Heat an ungreased heavy-based frying pan, add the whole tomatoes and garlic and char over a high heat or under a preheated grill. The skins of the vegetables should blacken and char, and the flesh inside should be tender. Alternatively, place the tomatoes and garlic cloves in a roasting tin and bake in a preheated oven at 190–200° C/375–400° F/Gas Mark 5–6 for about 40 minutes.

❷ Allow the tomatoes and garlic to cool, then remove the skins and chop roughly, combining them with any juices from the tin. Set aside.

❸ Poach the snapper in the stock over medium heat just until it is opaque and firmish. Remove from the heat and set aside.

❹ Heat the oil in a pan and cook the chopped onion until softened. Strain in the cooking liquid from the fish, then add the chopped tomatoes and garlic. Bring to the boil, then reduce the heat and simmer for about 5 minutes to combine the flavours. Add the serrano chillies.

❺ Divide chunks of the poached fish between soup bowls, ladle over the soup and serve with lime wedges for squeezing over.

 very easy

 serves 4

 15 minutes

 1 hour, 5 minutes

Provençale Fish Soup

INGREDIENTS

1 tbsp olive oil
2 onions, finely chopped
1 small leek, thinly sliced
1 small carrot, finely chopped
1 celery stick, finely chopped
1 small fennel bulb, finely chopped (optional)
3 garlic cloves, finely chopped
225 ml/8 fl oz dry white wine
400 g/14 oz canned tomatoes in juice
1 bay leaf
pinch of fennel seeds
2 strips orange rind
¼ tsp saffron threads
1.2 litres/2 pints water
350 g/12 oz skinless white fish fillets
salt and pepper
garlic croûtons, to serve

❶ Heat the oil in a large saucepan over a medium heat. Add the onions and cook for about 5 minutes, stirring frequently, until softened. Add the leek, carrot, celery, fennel and garlic, then continue cooking for 4–5 minutes, or until the leek is wilted.

❷ Add the wine and allow it to bubble for a minute. Add the tomatoes, bay leaf, fennel seeds, orange rind, saffron and water. Bring just to the boil, reduce the heat, then cover and cook gently, stirring occasionally, for 30 minutes.

❸ Add the fish and cook for an additional 20–30 minutes, or until it is very soft and flaky. Remove the bay leaf and orange rind if possible.

❹ Allow the soup to cool slightly, then transfer to a blender or food processor and purée until smooth, working in batches if necessary. (If using a food processor, strain off the cooking liquid and reserve. Purée the soup solids with enough cooking liquid to moisten them, then combine with the remaining liquid.)

❺ Return the soup to the saucepan. Taste and adjust the seasoning, if necessary, and simmer for 5–10 minutes, or until heated through. Ladle the soup into warm bowls and sprinkle with croûtons.

very easy

serves 4

15 minutes

1½ hours

Caribbean Green Seafood Soup

INGREDIENTS

150 g/5½ oz peeled
   medium prawns
200 g/7 oz skinless firm
   white fish fillets,
   cubed
¾ tsp ground coriander
¼ tsp ground cumin
1 tsp chilli paste, or to
   taste
3 tbsp fresh lemon juice,
   or to taste
1 tbsp butter
1 onion, halved and
   thinly sliced
2 large leeks, thinly
   sliced
3 garlic cloves, finely
   chopped
1 large potato, diced
1.2 litres/2 pints chicken
   or vegetable stock
250 g/9 oz spinach
   leaves
125 ml/4 fl oz coconut
   milk
salt and pepper

❶ Put the prawns and fish in a bowl with the coriander, cumin, chilli paste and lemon juice and leave to marinate.

❷ Melt the butter in a large saucepan over a medium heat. Add the onion and leeks, cover and cook for 10 minutes, stirring occasionally, until soft. Add the garlic and cook for 3–4 minutes.

❸ Add the potato and stock, together with a large pinch of salt, if using unsalted stock. Bring to the boil, reduce the heat, then cover and cook gently for 15–20 minutes, or until the potato is tender. Stir in the spinach and continue cooking, uncovered, for about 3 minutes, or until it is just wilted.

❹ Allow the soup to cool slightly, then transfer to a blender or food processor, working in batches if necessary. Purée the soup until smooth. (If using a food processor, strain off the cooking liquid and reserve. Purée the soup solids with enough cooking liquid to moisten them, then combine with the remaining liquid.)

❺ Return the soup to the saucepan and stir in the coconut milk. Add the fish and prawns with their marinade. Simmer over a medium-low heat for 8 minutes, stirring frequently, until the soup is heated through and the fish is cooked and flakes easily.

❻ Taste and adjust the seasoning, adding more chilli paste and/or lemon juice, if wished. Ladle into warm bowls and serve.

easy

serves 4

15 minutes,
plus 2 hours
to marinate

55 minutes

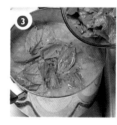

Garlic Fish Soup

❶ Heat the oil in a large saucepan over a medium-low heat. Add the onion, fennel, leek and garlic and cook for 4–5 minutes, stirring frequently, until the onion is softened.

❷ Add the wine and bubble briefly. Add the stock, rice, lemon rind and bay leaf. Bring to the boil, reduce the heat to medium–low and simmer for 20–25 minutes, or until the rice and vegetables are soft. Remove the lemon rind and bay leaf.

❸ Allow the soup to cool slightly, then transfer to a blender or food processor and purée until smooth, working in batches if necessary. (If using a food processor, strain off the cooking liquid and reserve. Purée the soup solids with enough cooking liquid to moisten them, then combine with the remaining liquid.)

❹ Return the soup to the saucepan and bring to a simmer. Add the fish to the soup, cover and continue simmering gently, stirring occasionally, for 4–5 minutes, or until the fish is cooked and begins to flake.

❺ Stir in the cream. Taste and adjust the seasoning, adding salt, if needed, and pepper. Ladle into warm bowls and serve sprinkled with parsley.

 very easy

 serves 4

 15 minutes

 50 minutes

Taramasalata with Pitta Wedges

INGREDIENTS

225 g/8 oz smoked
cod's roe
1 small onion, finely
chopped
1 garlic clove
55 g/2 oz fresh white
bread without crusts
finely grated rind of
1 lemon
4 tbsp lemon juice,
plus extra to taste,
if desired
150 ml/5 fl oz extra-
virgin olive oil
6 tbsp hot water
salt and pepper
hollowed-out tomatoes,
to serve
fresh flat-leaved parsley
sprigs, to garnish

PITTA WEDGES
2 pitta breads
olive oil, for brushing

❶ Remove the skin from the smoked cod's roe. Put the roe and onion in a food processor and process until well blended and smooth. Add the garlic and process again.

❷ Break the bread into the food processor, then add the lemon rind and 4 tablespoons of the lemon juice. Process again until the bread is well incorporated.

❸ With the motor running, gradually add the olive oil through the feed tube, as if making a mayonnaise. When all the oil is incorporated, add the hot water and process again. Add salt and pepper to taste, plus extra lemon juice if desired. Spoon into a bowl, then cover with clingfilm and chill until ready to serve.

❹ To make the pitta wedges, use a serrated knife to cut the pitta breads in half through the centre. Cut each half into 6–8 wedges, depending on the size. Place on a baking sheet and brush the inside surfaces of the wedges with olive oil.

❺ Bake in a preheated oven at 180° C/350° F/Gas Mark 4 for 20 minutes. Place on wire racks to cool.

❻ Spoon the taramasalata into the tomato shells, garnish with parsley and serve with the pitta wedges for dipping.

 extremely easy

 serves 4

 20 minutes

 20 minutes

16

Citrus-marinated Fish

INGREDIENTS

450 g/1 lb white-fleshed
   fish fillets, cut into
   bite-sized chunks
juice of 6–8 limes
2 or 3 ripe flavourful
   tomatoes, diced
3 fresh green chillies,
   such as jalapeño or
   serrano, deseeded
   and thinly sliced
½ tsp dried oregano
80 ml/3 fl oz extra-virgin
   olive oil
1 small onion, finely
   chopped
salt and pepper
fresh coriander, to serve

❶ Place the fish in a non-metallic dish, add the lime juice and mix well. Marinate in the refrigerator for 5 hours, or until the mixture looks opaque. Turn from time to time so that the lime juice permeates the fish.

❷ An hour before serving, add the tomatoes, chillies, oregano, olive oil and onion, then season with salt and pepper to taste.

❸ About 15 minutes before serving, remove from the refrigerator so that the olive oil comes to room temperature. Serve sprinkled with fresh coriander.

 extremely easy

 serves 4

 5 minutes,
plus 5 hours
to marinate

 0 minutes

COOK'S TIP
In this salad the fish is 'cooked' by the lime juice — do not leave too long, otherwise the texture will spoil.

Thai Fish Cakes with Hot Peanut Dip

INGREDIENTS

350 g/12 oz white fish
fillet without skin,
such as cod or
haddock
1 tbsp Thai fish sauce
2 tsp red curry paste
1 tbsp lime juice
1 garlic clove, crushed
4 dried kaffir lime
leaves, crumbled
1 egg white
3 tbsp chopped fresh
coriander
vegetable oil for
pan-frying
salad leaves, to serve

PEANUT DIP

1 small red chilli
1 tbsp light soy sauce
1 tbsp lime juice
1 tbsp soft light brown
sugar
3 tbsp chunky peanut
butter
4 tbsp coconut milk
salt and pepper

❶ Put the fish fillet in a food processor with the fish sauce, curry paste, lime juice, garlic, lime leaves and egg white and process until a smooth paste forms.

❷ Stir in the coriander and quickly process again until mixed. Divide the mixture into 8–10 pieces and roll into balls, then flatten to make round patties and set aside.

❸ For the dip, halve and deseed the chilli, then chop finely. Place in a small pan with the remaining dip ingredients and heat gently, stirring constantly, until well blended. Adjust the seasoning to taste.

❹ Pan-fry the fish cakes in batches for 3–4 minutes on each side, or until golden brown. Drain on kitchen paper and serve hot on a bed of salad leaves with the chilli-flavoured peanut dip.

 very easy

 serves 4

 15 minutes

 15–20 minutes

Smoked Mackerel Pâté

INGREDIENTS

*200 g/7 oz smoked
mackerel fillet*
*1 small, hot green chilli,
deseeded and
chopped*
1 garlic clove, chopped
3 tbsp coriander leaves
*150 ml/5 fl oz soured
cream*
*1 small red onion,
chopped*
2 tbsp lime juice
salt and pepper
*4 slices white bread,
crusts removed*

❶ Skin and flake the mackerel fillet, removing any small bones. Put the flesh in the bowl of a food processor along with the chilli, garlic, coriander and soured cream. Blend until smooth.

❷ Transfer the mixture to a bowl and mix in the onion and lime juice. Season to taste. The pâté will seem very soft at this stage, but it will firm up in the refrigerator. Refrigerate for several hours or overnight if possible.

❸ To make the melba toasts, place the trimmed bread slices under a preheated medium grill and toast lightly on both sides. Split the toasts in half horizontally, then cut each across diagonally to form 4 triangles per slice.

❹ Put the triangles, untoasted side up, under the grill and toast until golden and curled at the edges. Serve warm or cold with the smoked mackerel pâté.

extremely easy

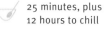
serves 4

25 minutes, plus
12 hours to chill

10 minutes

COOK'S TIP
This pâté is also
very good served
with crudities.

Light Meals & Salads

Fish dishes are ideal for light lunches or suppers – but they need not be dull. Instead of your usual sandwich, try a hearty Pan Bagna, packed with tuna, anchovies, olives and hard-boiled eggs layered with lettuce and tomatoes; a thick slice of multigrain bread topped with Smoked Haddock Salad; or Fish Tacos Ensenada-style – a kind of Mexican sandwich of chunks of fried white fish and cabbage salad, served in a soft tortilla instead of bread.

Pan Bagna

INGREDIENTS

40 cm/16 inch long loaf
of country bread,
thicker than a French
baguette
fruity extra-virgin
olive oil
black or green olive
tapenade (optional)

FILLING
2 eggs
50 g/1¾ oz anchovy
fillets in oil
about 85 g/3 oz black or
green olives, stoned
and chopped
lettuce or rocket leaves,
rinsed and patted dry
about 4 plum tomatoes,
sliced
200 g/7 oz canned tuna
in brine, well drained
and flaked

❶ To make the filling, start by hard-boiling the eggs. Bring a saucepan of water to the boil. Add the eggs and return to the boil, then continue boiling for 12 minutes. Drain and immediately plunge into a bowl of ice-cold water to stop the cooking.

❷ Peel the boiled eggs and cut into slices. Drain the anchovy fillets well, then cut them in half lengthways if large. Stone the olives and slice in half. Set aside.

❸ Using a serrated knife, slice the loaf in half lengthways. Remove about 1 cm/½ inch of the crumb from the top and bottom, leaving a border all around both halves.

❹ Generously brush both halves with the olive oil. Spread with tapenade, if you like a strong, robust flavour. Arrange a layer of lettuce or rocket leaves on the bottom half.

❺ Add layers of hard-boiled egg slices, tomato slices, olives, anchovies and tuna, sprinkling with olive oil and adding lettuce or rocket leaves between the layers. Make the filling as thick as you like.

❻ Place the other bread half on top and press down firmly. Wrap tightly in clingfilm and place on a board or plate that will fit in your refrigerator. Weight down and chill for several hours. To serve, slice into 4 equal portions, tying with string to secure in place, if desired.

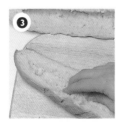

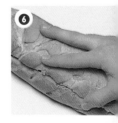

very easy

serves 4

20 minutes

12 minutes

Prawn Skewers with Tomato Salsa

INGREDIENTS

32 large tiger prawns
olive oil, for brushing
skordalia or aioli,
   to serve

MARINADE
125 ml/4 fl oz extra-
   virgin olive oil
2 tbsp lemon juice
1 tsp finely chopped
   red chilli
1 tsp balsamic vinegar
pepper

TOMATO SALSA
2 large sun-ripened
   tomatoes, skinned,
   cored, deseeded
   and chopped
4 spring onions, white
   parts only, very finely
   chopped
1 red pepper, skinned,
   deseeded and
   chopped
1 orange or yellow
   pepper, skinned,
   deseeded, and
   chopped
1 tbsp extra-virgin
   olive oil
2 tsp balsamic vinegar
4 sprigs fresh basil

❶ To make the marinade, place all the ingredients in a non-metallic bowl and whisk together. Set aside.

❷ To prepare the prawns, break off the heads. Peel off the shells, leaving the tails intact. Using a small knife, make a slit along the back and remove the thin black vein. Add the prawns to the marinade and stir until well coated. Cover and chill for 15 minutes.

❸ Make the salsa. Put all the ingredients, except the basil, in a non-metallic bowl and toss together. Season to taste with salt and pepper.

❹ Thread 4 prawns onto a metal skewer, bending each in half. Repeat with 7 more skewers. Brush with marinade.

❺ Brush a grill rack with oil. Place the skewers on the rack, then position under a preheated hot grill, about 7.5 cm/3 inches from the heat; cook for 1 minute. Turn the skewers over, brush again and continue to cook for 1–1½ minutes, or until the prawns turn pink and opaque.

❻ Tear the basil leaves and toss with the salsa. Arrange each skewer on a plate with some salsa and garnish with parsley. Serve with skordalia or aioli dip.

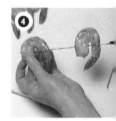

easy

serves 4

25 minutes,
plus 15 minutes
to marinate

5 minutes

Pasta with Tuna Lemon

INGREDIENTS

55 g/2 oz butter, diced
300 ml/10 fl oz double
   cream
4 tbsp lemon juice
1 tbsp grated lemon rind
½ tsp anchovy essence
400 g/14 oz dried fusilli
200 g/7 oz canned tuna
   in olive oil, drained
   and flaked
salt and pepper

TO GARNISH
2 tbsp finely chopped
   fresh parsley
grated lemon rind

❶ Bring a large saucepan of lightly salted water to the boil. Melt the butter in a large frying pan. Stir in the double cream and lemon juice and simmer, stirring, for about 2 minutes, or until slightly thickened.

❷ Stir in the lemon rind and anchovy essence. Meanwhile, cook the pasta for 10–12 minutes, or according to the instructions on the packet, until just al dente. Drain well.

❸ Add the sauce to the pasta and toss until well coated. Add the tuna and gently toss until well blended but not too broken up.

❹ Season to taste with salt and pepper. Transfer to a serving platter and garnish with the parsley and lemon rind. Grind some pepper over the dish and serve at once.

 extremely easy

 serves 4

 5 minutes

 10–12 minutes

VARIATIONS

For a vegetarian version, replace the tuna and anchovy essence with some stoned olives. Add a pinch of dried chilli flakes to the sauce or tear basil leaves into thin strips and stir into the dish before serving.

Crab Risotto with Roasted Peppers

INGREDIENTS

2–3 large red peppers
3 tbsp olive oil
1 onion, finely chopped
1 small fennel bulb,
    finely chopped
2 celery sticks, finely
    chopped
¼–½ tsp cayenne
    pepper, or to taste
350 g/12 oz arborio or
    carnaroli rice
800 g/1 lb 12 oz canned
    Italian peeled plum
    tomatoes, drained
    and chopped
50 ml/2 fl oz dry white
    vermouth (optional)
1.5 litres/2¾ pints fish
    or light chicken stock,
    simmering
450 g/1 lb fresh cooked
    crab meat (white and
    dark meat)
50 ml/2 fl oz lemon juice
2–4 tbsp chopped fresh
    parsley or chervil
salt and pepper

❶ Grill the peppers until the skins are charred. Transfer to a plastic bag and twist to seal. When cool enough to handle, peel off the charred skins, working over a bowl to catch the juices. Remove the cores and seeds; chop the flesh and set aside, reserving the juices.

❷ Heat the olive oil in a large heavy-based saucepan. Add the onion, fennel and celery and cook for 2–3 minutes, or until the vegetables are softened. Add the cayenne and rice and cook, stirring frequently, for about 2 minutes, or until the rice is translucent and well coated.

❸ Stir in the tomatoes and vermouth, if using. The liquid will bubble and steam rapidly. When the liquid is almost absorbed, add a ladleful (about 225 ml/8 fl oz) of the simmering stock. Cook, stirring constantly, until the liquid is completely absorbed.

❹ Continue adding the stock, about half a ladleful at a time, allowing each addition to be absorbed before adding the next. This should take 20–25 minutes. The risotto should have a creamy consistency and the rice should be tender but firm to the bite.

❺ Stir in the red peppers and juices, the crab meat, lemon juice, and parsley or chervil, then heat. Season with salt and pepper to taste. Serve immediately.

easy

serves 4

10 minutes

40 minutes

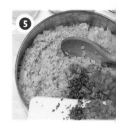

Chinese Fried Rice

INGREDIENTS

2–3 tbsp groundnut or
vegetable oil

2 onions, halved and cut
lengthways into thin
wedges

2 garlic cloves, thinly
sliced

2.5 cm/1 inch piece fresh
ginger root, peeled,
and cut into slivers

200 g/7 oz cooked ham,
thinly sliced

300 g/10½ oz cooked, cold
long-grain white rice

250 g/9 oz cooked peeled
prawns

115 g/4 oz canned water
chestnuts, sliced

3 eggs

3 tsp sesame oil

4–6 spring onions,
diagonally sliced into
1 inch/2.5 cm pieces

2 tbsp dark soy sauce

1 tbsp sweet chilli sauce

2 tbsp chopped fresh
coriander

salt and pepper

❶ Heat 2–3 tablespoons groundnut oil in a wok or large, deep frying pan until very hot. Add the onions and stir-fry for 2 minutes, or until beginning to soften. Add the garlic and ginger and stir-fry for a further minute. Add the ham strips and stir to combine.

❷ Add the cold cooked rice and stir to mix with the vegetables and ham. Stir in the prawns and the water chestnuts. Stir in 2 tablespoons of water and cover the pan quickly. Continue to cook for 2 minutes, shaking the pan occasionally to prevent sticking and to let the rice heat through.

❸ Beat the eggs with 1 teaspoon of the sesame oil and season with salt and pepper. Make a well in the centre of the rice mixture then add the eggs and immediately stir, gradually drawing the rice into the eggs.

❹ Stir in the spring onions, soy sauce and chilli sauce and stir-fry; stir in a little more water if the rice looks dry or is sticking. Drizzle in the remaining sesame oil and stir. Season to taste with salt and pepper.

❺ Remove from the heat and wipe the edge of the wok or frying pan, then sprinkle with the coriander. Serve immediately.

 very easy

 serves 4

 25 minutes

 15 minutes

Fish Tacos Ensenada Style

INGREDIENTS

450 g/1 lb firm-fleshed
   white fish, such as
   red snapper or cod
¼ tsp dried oregano
¼ tsp ground cumin
1 tsp mild chilli powder
2 or 3 garlic cloves,
   finely chopped
3 tbsp plain flour
vegetable oil, for frying
¼ red cabbage, thinly
   sliced or shredded
juice of 2 limes
hot pepper sauce or
   salsa to taste
8 soft corn tortillas
1 tbsp chopped fresh
   coriander
½ onion, chopped
   (optional)
salt and pepper
salsa of your choice

❶ Place the fish on a plate and sprinkle with half the oregano, cumin, chilli powder, garlic, and salt and pepper, then dust with the flour.

❷ Heat the oil in a frying pan until it is smoking, then cook the fish in several batches until it is golden on the outside, and just tender in the middle. Remove from the frying pan and place on kitchen paper to drain.

❸ Combine the cabbage with the remaining oregano, cumin, chilli and garlic, then stir in the lime juice, and salt and hot pepper sauce to taste. Set aside.

❹ Heat the tortillas in an ungreased nonstick frying pan, sprinkling with a few drops of water as they heat; wrap the tortillas in a clean tea towel as you work to keep them warm. Alternatively, heat through in a stack in the frying pan, alternating the top and bottom tortillas so that they warm evenly.

❺ Place some of the warm fried fish in each tortilla, along with a big spoonful of the cabbage salad. Sprinkle with fresh coriander and onion, if using. Add salsa to taste and serve at once.

 extremely easy

 serves 4

 5 minutes

 25–30 minutes

Hot-Smoked Trout Tart

INGREDIENTS

175 g/6 oz plain flour
1 tsp salt
80 g/3 oz butter, cut into
    small pieces
1 egg yolk

FILLING
25 g/1 oz butter
1 small onion, finely
    chopped
1 tsp green peppercorns
    in brine, drained and
    roughly chopped
2 tsp stem ginger,
    drained
2 tsp stem ginger syrup
225 g/8 oz hot-smoked
    trout fillets, flaked
3 egg yolks
100 ml/3½ fl oz crème
    fraîche
100 ml/3½ fl oz
    double cream
1 tbsp chopped fresh
    parsley
1 tbsp chopped fresh
    chives
salt and pepper

❶ Sift together the flour and salt. Add the butter and rub in well with your fingertips until the mixture resembles coarse breadcrumbs. Add the egg yolk and about 2 tablespoons of cold water, to make a firm dough. Knead briefly, wrap in clingfilm and refrigerate for 30 minutes.

❷ Meanwhile, make the filling. Melt the butter in a frying pan and add the onion. Cook gently for 8–10 minutes until softened but not coloured. Remove from the heat and stir in the peppercorns, ginger, ginger syrup and flaked trout. Set aside.

❸ Remove the pastry from the refrigerator and roll out thinly. Use to line a 23 cm/9 inch flan tin or dish. Prick the base at regular intervals with a fork. Line the pastry with foil or baking parchment and baking beans. Bake in a preheated oven at 200°C/400°F/Gas Mark 6 for 12 minutes. Remove the foil or baking parchment and beans and bake for an additional 10 minutes until light golden and dry. Remove from the oven and allow to cool slightly. Reduce the oven temperature to 180°C/350°F/Gas Mark 4. Spread the trout mixture over the base of the pastry.

❹ Mix together the egg yolks, crème fraîche, cream, parsley, chives and seasoning. Pour this mixture over the trout mixture to cover. Bake in the preheated oven for 35–40 minutes until just set and golden. Remove from the oven and allow to cool slightly before serving with a mixed green salad or green vegetable.

 easy

 serves 4

 40 minutes, plus 30 minutes to chill dough

 52 minutes

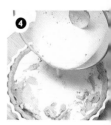

Smoked Haddock Salad

INGREDIENTS

350 g/12 oz smoked
   haddock fillet
4 tbsp olive oil
1 tbsp lemon juice
2 tbsp soured cream
1 tbsp hot water
2 tbsp chopped fresh
   chives
1 plum tomato, peeled,
   deseeded, and diced
8 quail's eggs
4 thick slices multigrain
   bread
115 g/4 oz mixed salad
   leaves
chives, to garnish
salt and pepper

extremely easy

serves 4

10 minutes

10 minutes

❶ Fill a large frying pan with water and bring to the boil. Add the smoked haddock fillet, cover and remove from the heat. Leave for 10 minutes, or until the fish is tender. Lift from the water, drain and leave until cool enough to handle. Flake the flesh, removing any small bones. Set aside. Discard the poaching water.

❷ Whisk together the olive oil, lemon juice, soured cream, hot water, chives and seasoning. Stir in the tomato. Set aside.

❸ Bring a small saucepan of water to the boil. Carefully lower the quail's eggs into the water. Cook the eggs for 3–4 minutes from when the water returns to the boil (3 minutes for a slightly soft centre, 4 minutes for a firm centre). Drain immediately and refresh under cold running water. Carefully peel the eggs, then cut in half lengthways and set aside.

❹ Toast the multigrain bread and cut each across diagonally to form 4 triangles. Arrange 2 halves on 4 serving plates. Top with the salad leaves, then the flaked fish and finally the quail's eggs. Spoon over the dressing and garnish with a few extra chives.

COOK'S TIP

When buying smoked haddock, and smoked fish in general, look for undyed fish, which is always superior in quality.

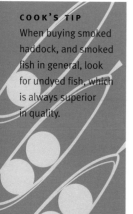

Salade Niçoise

INGREDIENTS

3 large eggs
250 g/9 oz French
    beans, topped
    and tailed
250 g/9 oz small waxy
    potatoes, such as
    Charlottes, scrubbed
    and halved
1 large, sun-ripened
    tomato, cut into
    eighths
1 large tuna steak,
    about 350 g/12 oz
    and 2 cm/¾ inch
    thick, seared
70 g/2½ oz Provençale-
    style olives or plain
    black olives
50 g/1¾ oz canned
    anchovy fillets in oil,
    drained
1 tbsp chopped fresh
    flat-leaved parsley

GARLIC VINAIGRETTE
125 ml/4 fl oz extra-
    virgin olive oil
3 tbsp red or white wine
    vinegar
½ tsp sugar
½ tsp Dijon mustard
2 garlic cloves, crushed
salt and pepper

❶ To make the vinaigrette, put all the ingredients in a screw-top jar and shake until blended. Season to taste, then set aside.

❷ Bring 3 pans of water to the boil. Add the eggs to one pan and bring back to the boil, then cook for 12 minutes. Drain immediately and run under cold running water to stop more cooking.

❸ Put the beans and potatoes into separate pans of boiling water. Blanch the beans for 3 minutes, then drain and transfer to a large bowl. Shake the dressing and pour it over the beans.

❹ Continue to cook the potatoes until they are tender, then drain and add to the beans and dressing while they are still hot. Allow the potatoes and beans to cool in the dressing.

❺ Add the tomato pieces to the vegetables in the dressing, then break the tuna into large chunks. Toss gently with the other ingredients.

❻ Peel the hard-boiled eggs and cut each into quarters lengthways.

❼ Mound the tuna and vegetables on a serving platter. Arrange the egg quarters around the side. Scatter the olives over the salad, then arrange the anchovies in a lattice on top. Cover and chill.

❽ About 15 minutes before serving, remove the salad from the refrigerator and allow it to come to room temperature. Sprinkle with parsley and serve.

 very easy

 serves 4

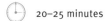 20 minutes

20–25 minutes

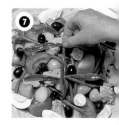

Lobster Salad

INGREDIENTS

2 raw lobster tails
salt and pepper

LEMON-DILL
MAYONNAISE
1 large lemon
1 large egg yolk
½ tsp Dijon mustard
150 ml/5 fl oz olive oil
1 tbsp chopped fresh dill

TO GARNISH
radicchio leaves
lemon wedges
fresh dill sprigs

 extremely easy

 serves 4

 20 minutes

6 minutes

❶ To make the lemon-dill mayonnaise, finely grate the rind from the lemon and squeeze the juice. Beat the egg yolk in a small bowl and beat in the mustard and 1 teaspoon of the lemon juice.

❷ Using a balloon whisk or electric mixer, beat in the olive oil, drop by drop, until a thick mayonnaise forms. Stir in half the lemon rind and 1 tablespoon of the juice.

❸ Season with salt and pepper, and add more lemon juice if desired. Stir in the dill and cover with clingfilm. Place in the refrigerator to chill until required.

❹ Bring a large saucepan of salted water to the boil. Add the lobster tails and continue to cook for 6 minutes, or until the flesh is opaque and the shells are red. Drain immediately and leave to cool completely.

❺ Remove the lobster flesh from the shells and cut into bite-sized pieces. Arrange the radicchio leaves on individual plates and top with the lobster flesh. Place a spoonful of the lemon-dill mayonnaise on the side. Garnish with lemon wedges and dill sprigs and serve.

COOK'S TIP

Use pasteurized egg products, available where eggs are sold, to minimize the risk of salmonella.

Prawn Salad & Toasted Rice

INGREDIENTS

225 g/8 oz cooked
 prawns, with tail
 shells left on
2 tbsp sunflower oil
cayenne pepper
1 tbsp long-grain white
 rice
1 large head cos lettuce
 with outer leaves
 removed
½ small cucumber,
 lightly peeled,
 deseeded and thinly
 sliced
1 small bunch chives,
 sliced into 2.5 cm/
 1 inch pieces
handful of fresh mint
 leaves
salt and pepper

DRESSING
50 ml/2 fl oz rice vinegar
1 red chilli, deseeded
 and thinly sliced
7.5 cm/3 inch piece
 lemon-grass stalk,
 crushed
juice of 1 lime
2 tbsp Thai fish sauce
2 tbsp water
1 tsp sugar, or to taste

❶ Split each prawn in half lengthways, leaving the tail attached to one half. Remove any dark intestinal veins and pat dry. Sprinkle with a little salt and cayenne pepper.

❷ To make the dressing, combine the vinegar with the chilli and lemon-grass. Leave to marinate.

❸ Heat the oil in a wok or heavy-based frying pan over a high heat. Add the rice and stir until brown and richly fragrant. Pour into a mortar and cool completely. Crush gently with a pestle until coarse crumbs form.

❹ Stir-fry the prawns in the cleaned wok for 1 minute, or until warm. Transfer to a plate and season with pepper.

❺ Tear or shred the lettuce into large bite-sized pieces and transfer to a shallow salad bowl. Add the cucumber, chives and mint leaves and toss to combine.

❻ Remove the lemon-grass and most of the chilli slices from the rice vinegar and whisk in the lime juice, fish sauce, water and sugar. Pour most of the dressing over the salad and toss. Top with the prawns and drizzle with the remaining dressing. Sprinkle with the toasted rice and serve.

 very easy

 serves 4

 25 minutes

 6 minutes

Thai Noodle Salad with Prawns

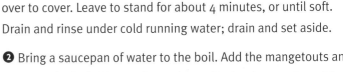

INGREDIENTS

*85 g/3 oz rice vermicelli
or rice sticks*
*175 g/6 oz mangetouts,
cut crossways in half,
if large*
5 tbsp lime juice
4 tbsp Thai fish sauce
1 tbsp sugar, or to taste
*2.5 cm/1 inch piece fresh
ginger root, peeled
and finely chopped*
*1 fresh red chili,
deseeded and thinly
sliced on the
diagonal*
*4 tbsp chopped fresh
coriander or mint,
plus extra for
garnishing*
*10 cm/4 inch piece of
cucumber, peeled,
deseeded and diced*
*2 spring onions, thinly
sliced on the
diagonal*
*16–20 large cooked,
peeled prawns*
*2 tbsp chopped
unsalted peanuts or
cashews (optional)*
*4 whole cooked prawns
and lemon slices,
to garnish*

❶ Put the rice noodles in a large bowl and pour enough hot water over to cover. Leave to stand for about 4 minutes, or until soft. Drain and rinse under cold running water; drain and set aside.

❷ Bring a saucepan of water to the boil. Add the mangetouts and return to the boil. Simmer for 1 minute. Drain, rinse under cold running water until cold, then drain and set aside.

❸ In a large bowl, whisk together the lime juice, fish sauce, sugar, ginger, chilli and coriander. Stir in the cucumber and spring onions. Add the drained noodles, mangetouts and the prawns. Toss the salad gently together.

❹ Divide the noodle salad among 4 large plates. Sprinkle with chopped coriander and the peanuts (if using), then garnish each plate with a whole prawn and a lemon slice. Serve immediately.

 extremely easy

 serves 4

15 minutes

 5 minutes, plus 4 minutes to stand

Warm Salad of Tuna & Tomatoes with Ginger Dressing

INGREDIENTS

55 g/2 oz Chinese
   cabbage, shredded
3 tbsp rice wine
2 tbsp Thai fish sauce
1 tbsp finely shredded
   fresh ginger
1 garlic clove, finely
   chopped
½ small bird's eye red
   chilli, finely chopped
2 tsp soft light brown
   sugar
2 tbsp lime juice
400 g/14 oz fresh tuna
   steak
sunflower oil for
   brushing
125 g/4½ oz cherry
   tomatoes
roughly chopped fresh
   mint leaves, to
   garnish

extremely easy

serves 4

10 minutes

15 minutes

❶ Place a small pile of the shredded Chinese cabbage on serving plates. Place the rice wine, fish sauce, ginger, garlic, chilli, brown sugar and 1 tablespoon of lime juice in a screw-top jar and shake well to combine evenly.

❷ Cut the tuna into strips of an even thickness. Sprinkle with the remaining lime juice.

❸ Brush a griddle or wide frying pan with the oil and heat until very hot. Arrange the tuna strips on the griddle and cook until just firm and light golden, turning once. Remove and set aside.

❹ Add the tomatoes to the griddle and cook over a high heat until lightly browned. Spoon the tuna and tomatoes over the Chinese cabbage and spoon over the dressing. Scatter with chopped fresh mint and serve warm.

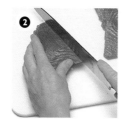

COOK'S TIP
You can make a quick version of this dish using canned tuna. Just drain and flake the tuna, omit steps 2 and 3, then continue as in the recipe.

Caesar Salad

INGREDIENTS

1 large cos lettuce or
2 hearts of cos
4 anchovies, drained
and halved
lengthways
Parmesan shavings,
to garnish

DRESSING
2 garlic cloves, crushed
1½ tsp Dijon mustard
1 tsp Worcestershire
sauce
4 anchovies in olive oil,
drained and chopped
1 egg yolk
1 tbsp lemon juice
150 ml/5 fl oz olive oil
4 tbsp freshly grated
Parmesan cheese
salt and pepper

CROÛTONS
4 thick slices day-old
bread
2 tbsp olive oil
1 garlic clove, crushed

❶ Make the dressing. In a food processor or blender, put the garlic, mustard, Worcestershire sauce, anchovies, egg yolk, lemon juice and seasoning, then blend for 30 seconds, or until foaming. Add the olive oil, drop by drop until the mixture begins to thicken, then in a steady stream until the oil is incorporated. Scrape out of the food processor or blender. Add some hot water if the dressing is too thick. Stir in the grated Parmesan cheese. Season to taste, then set aside in the refrigerator until required.

❷ For the croûtons, cut the bread into 2.5 cm/1 inch cubes. Toss with the oil and garlic in a bowl. Transfer to a baking sheet in a single layer. Bake in a preheated oven at 180°C/350°F/Gas Mark 4 for 15–20 minutes, stirring occasionally, until the croûtons are browned and crisp. Remove from the oven and allow to cool.

❸ Separate the lettuce or lettuce hearts into individual leaves and wash. Tear into pieces and spin dry in a salad spinner. Alternatively, dry the leaves on clean kitchen paper. (Excess moisture will dilute the dressing and make the salad taste watery.) Transfer to a plastic bag and refrigerate until needed.

❹ To assemble the salad, put the lettuce pieces into a large serving bowl. Add the dressing and toss thoroughly until all the leaves are coated. Top with the halved anchovies, croûtons and Parmesan shavings. Serve at once while still hot.

 very easy

 serves 4

 20 minutes

 15–20 minutes

Main Meals

One of the easiest ways to cook fish is in the oven, wrapped in foil or baking paper, or simply topped with a sauce and baked. Fish Baked with Limes sandwiches white fish, drenched in lime juice, between a tasty mixture of garlic, onions, chillies and coriander – and is ready to serve in 30 minutes. Smoked Fish Pie takes a little longer, but this comforting dish, topped with cheese-flavoured rösti potatoes, is worth the extra effort.

Seafood Stew

INGREDIENTS

225 g/8 oz clams
700 g/1 lb 9 oz mixed
  fish, such as sea
  bass, skate, red
  snapper, rock fish,
  and any
  Mediterranean fish
  you can find
12–18 tiger prawns
about 3 tbsp olive oil
1 large onion, finely
  chopped
2 garlic cloves, very
  finely chopped
2 sun-ripened
  tomatoes, halved,
  deseeded and
  chopped
700 ml/1¼ pints good-
  quality, ready-made
  chilled fish stock
1 tbsp tomato purée
1 tsp fresh thyme leaves
pinch of saffron threads
pinch of sugar
salt and pepper
finely chopped fresh
  parsley, to garnish

❶ Soak the clams in a bowl of lightly salted water for 30 minutes. Rinse them under cold, running water and lightly scrub to remove any sand from the shells. Discard any broken clams or open clams that do not shut when firmly tapped with the back of a knife, because these will be unsafe to eat.

❷ Prepare the fish as necessary, removing any skin and bones, then cut into bite-sized chunks.

❸ To prepare the prawns, break off the heads. Peel off the shells, leaving the tails intact, if desired. Using a small knife, make a slit along the back of each and remove the thin black vein. Set all the seafood aside.

❹ Heat the oil in a large pan. Add the onion and cook for 5 minutes, stirring. Add the garlic and cook for a further 2 minutes, or until the onion is soft, but not brown.

❺ Add the tomatoes, stock, tomato purée, thyme leaves, saffron threads and sugar, then bring to the boil, stirring to dissolve the tomato purée. Lower the heat, cover and simmer for 15 minutes. Adjust the seasoning.

❻ Add the seafood and simmer until the clams open and the fish flakes easily. Discard the bouquet garni and any clams that do not open. Garnish and serve at once.

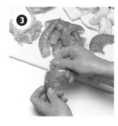

 easy

 serves 4

 20 minutes,
  plus 30 minutes
  to soak

 35–40 minutes

Swordfish à la Maltese

INGREDIENTS

1 tbsp fennel seeds
2 tbsp fruity extra-virgin olive oil, plus extra for brushing and drizzling
2 large onions, thinly sliced
1 small garlic clove, crushed
4 swordfish steaks, about 175 g/6 oz each
1 large lemon, cut in half
2 large sun-ripened tomatoes, finely chopped
4 sprigs fresh thyme
salt and pepper

❶ Place the fennel seeds in a dry frying pan over a medium-high heat and toast, stirring, until they give off their aroma, watching carefully so that they do not burn. Immediately pour out of the pan onto a plate. Set aside.

❷ Heat 2 tablespoons of the olive oil in the frying pan. Add the onions and cook for 5 minutes, stirring occasionally. Add the garlic and continue cooking the onions until very soft and tender, but not brown. Remove the frying pan from the heat.

❸ Cut out four 30 cm/12 inch rounds of baking paper. Very lightly brush the centre of each paper round with olive oil. Equally divide the onions between the paper rounds, flattening them out to about the size of the fish steaks.

❹ Top the onions in each parcel with a swordfish steak. Squeeze lemon juice over the fish steaks and drizzle with a little olive oil. Scatter the tomatoes over the top, add a sprig of thyme to each, and season with salt and pepper to taste.

❺ Fold the edges of the paper together, scrunching them tightly so that no juices escape during cooking. Place on a baking sheet and cook in a preheated oven at 200°C/400°F/Gas Mark 6 for 20 minutes.

❻ To test if the fish is cooked, open one package and pierce the flesh with a knife — it should flake easily. Serve straight from the paper packages.

 very easy

 serves 4

10 minutes

 30 minutes

Mediterranean Monkfish

INGREDIENTS

550 g/1 lb 4 oz vine-
ripened cherry
tomatoes, a mixture
of yellow and red,
if available
2 monkfish fillets, about
350 g/12 oz each
8 tbsp pesto sauce

extremely easy

serves 4

15 minutes

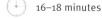
16–18 minutes

1 Cut the tomatoes in half and scatter, cut-sides up, on the base of an ovenproof serving dish. Set aside.

2 Using your fingers, rub off the thin grey membrane that covers the monkfish.

3 If the skin has not been removed, place the fish skin-side down on the work surface. Loosen enough skin at one end of the fillet so you can grip it. Work from the front of the fillet to the back. Insert the knife, almost flat, and using a gentle sawing action, remove the skin. Rinse the fillets well and dry with kitchen paper.

4 Place the fillets on top of the tomatoes, tucking the thin end under, if necessary (see Cook's Tip). Spread 4 tablespoons of the pesto sauce over each fillet and season with pepper.

5 Cover the dish tightly with foil, shiny-side down. Place in a preheated oven at 230°C/450°F/Gas Mark 8 and roast for 16–18 minutes, or until the fish is cooked through, the flesh flakes easily and the tomatoes are dissolving into a thick sauce.

6 Adjust the seasoning, if necessary. Garnish with basil sprigs and serve at once with new potatoes.

COOK'S TIP

Monkfish fillets are often cut from the tail, which means one end is much thinner than the rest and prone to overcooking. If you can't get fillets that are the same thickness, fold the thin end under for even cooking.

Wrapped Red Mullet with Stewed Peppers & Fennel

INGREDIENTS

3 tbsp olive oil, plus
    extra for rubbing
2 large red peppers,
    cored, deseeded and
    thinly sliced
2 large bulbs fennel,
    trimmed and thinly
    sliced
1 large clove garlic,
    crushed
8 sprigs fresh thyme,
    plus extra for
    garnishing
20–24 vine leaves in
    brine
1 lemon
4 red mullet, about
    225 g/8 oz each,
    scaled and gutted
salt and pepper

 very easy

 serves 4

 15 minutes

 35 minutes

❶ Heat the oil in a large frying pan over medium-low heat. Add the peppers, fennel, garlic and 4 sprigs of thyme and stir together. Cook, stirring occasionally, for about 20 minutes, or until the vegetables are cooked thoroughly and are very soft, but not browned.

❷ Meanwhile, rinse the vine leaves under cold, running water and pat dry with kitchen paper. Slice 4 thin slices off the lemon, then cut each slice in half. Finely grate the rind of ½ the lemon.

❸ Stuff the mullet cavities with the lemon slices and remaining thyme sprigs. Rub a little olive oil on each fish and sprinkle with the lemon rind. Season with salt and pepper to taste.

❹ Wrap 5 or 6 vine leaves around each mullet, depending on the size of the mullet, to completely enclose. Put the mullet on top of the fennel and peppers. Cover the pan and cook over medium-low heat for 12–15 minutes, or until the fish is cooked through and the flesh flakes easily when tested with the tip of a knife.

❺ Transfer the cooked fish to individual plates and spoon the fennel and peppers alongside. Garnish with thyme sprigs and serve.

COOK'S TIP
Replace the red mullet with tuna or swordfish steaks, cooking them for 8–10 minutes, depending on the thickness and how well done you like your fish cooked.

Moules Marinara

INGREDIENTS

2 kg/4 lb 8 oz live
    mussels
4 tbsp olive oil
4–6 large garlic cloves,
    halved
800 g/28 oz canned
    chopped
    tomatoes
300 ml/10 fl oz dry white
    wine
2 tbsp finely chopped
    fresh flat-leaved
    parsley, plus extra for
    garnishing
1 tbsp finely chopped
    fresh oregano
salt and pepper
French bread, to serve

❶ Soak the mussels in a bowl of lightly salted water for 30 minutes. Rinse them under cold, running water and lightly scrub to remove any sand from the shells. Using a small sharp knife, remove the 'beards' from the shells.

❷ Discard any broken mussels or open mussels that do not shut when firmly tapped with the back of a knife. This indicates that they are dead and could cause food poisoning if eaten. Rinse the mussels again, then set aside in a colander.

❸ Heat the olive oil in a large saucepan or stockpot over medium-high heat. Add the garlic and fry, stirring, for about 3 minutes to flavour the oil. Using a slotted spoon, remove the garlic from the pan.

❹ Add the tomatoes and their juice, the wine, parsley and oregano and bring to the boil, stirring. Lower the heat, then cover and simmer for 5 minutes to allow the flavours to blend.

❺ Add the mussels, cover the pan and simmer for 5–8 minutes, shaking the pan regularly, until the mussels open. Using a slotted spoon, transfer the mussels to serving bowls, discarding any that are not open.

❻ Season the sauce, then ladle it over the mussels. Sprinkle with extra chopped parsley, and serve at once with plenty of French bread to mop up the delicious juices.

 easy

 serves 4

 10–15 minutes,
plus 30 minutes
to soak

 20 minutes

Seared Scallops with Champagne Saffron Sauce

 very easy

 serves 4

 5 minutes

 25–30 minutes

❶ Heat a large dry frying pan, preferably non-stick, over high heat. Add the saffron threads and toast just until they start to give off their aroma. Immediately pour onto a plate and set aside.

❷ Melt half the butter in the frying pan. Add half the scallops and fry for 2 minutes. Turn and fry for a further 1½–2 minutes, or until the scallops are set and the flesh is opaque all the way through when you pierce one with a knife (see Cook's Tip).

❸ Transfer the scallops to a hot dish, then cover and keep warm while cooking the rest in the same way, adding more butter as necessary.

❹ Add the saffron to the cooking juices and pour in the champagne, cream and any reserved scallop juices, stirring. Bring to the boil, then lower the heat slightly and simmer for about 10 minutes, or until reduced to a consistency that coats the back of a spoon.

❺ Add freshly squeezed lemon juice and salt and pepper to taste. Return the scallops to the pan and stir until just heated through. Transfer to 4 plates and garnish with parsley. Serve at once.

COOK'S TIP

The exact cooking time depends on the thickness of the scallops. If the scallops are thinner, cook them for only 1½ minutes on each side. Take great care not to overcook.

Kedgeree

INGREDIENTS

675 g/1½ lb thick,
    undyed smoked
    haddock or cod fillets
milk, for poaching
2 bay leaves
1 tbsp vegetable oil
55 g/2 oz butter
1 onion, finely chopped
1 tsp hot curry powder,
    or to taste
1 tsp dry mustard
    powder
300 g/10½ oz basmati
    rice
850 ml/1½ pints water
2 small leeks, trimmed
    and cut into
    5 mm/¼ inch slices
2 tbsp chopped fresh
    flat-leaved parsley or
    coriander
a squeeze of lemon juice
3 or 4 hard-boiled eggs,
    peeled and quartered
salt and pepper
lemon quarters, to serve

❶ Put the fish in a frying pan and pour in enough milk to just cover; add the bay leaves. Bring to the boil, then simmer gently, covered, for about 4 minutes. Remove from the heat and leave to stand, covered, for about 10 minutes.

❷ Using a slotted spoon, transfer the fish to a plate and cover loosely; set aside. Reserve the milk, discarding the bay leaves.

❸ Heat the oil and half the butter in a large pan, then add the onion and cook for about 2 minutes, or until soft. Stir in the curry powder and the mustard powder and cook for 1 minute.

❹ Add the rice and stir for 2 minutes, or until well coated. Add the water and bring to the boil; stir and reduce the heat to very low. Cook, covered, for 20–25 minutes, or until the rice is tender and the water absorbed.

❺ Melt the remaining butter in a flameproof casserole, add the leeks and cook for 4 minutes, or until soft. Fork the leeks into the rice. Add 2–3 tablespoons of the reserved milk to moisten.

❻ Flake the fish off the skin into large pieces and fold into the rice. Stir in the parsley and lemon juice, then season with salt and pepper. Add more milk, if desired, then add the egg quarters. Serve with lemon quarters.

 very easy

 serves 4

 15 minutes

 50 minutes,
plus 10 minutes
to poach

Salmon Coulibiac

INGREDIENTS

100 g/3½ oz butter, plus
    extra 25 g/1 oz butter,
    melted
2 onions, finely
    chopped
115 g/4 oz long-grain
    white rice
750 g/1 lb 10 oz skinned
    salmon fillet,
    poached in water,
    cooking liquid
    reserved
150 g/5½ oz mushrooms,
    thinly sliced
85 g/3 oz cooked
    spinach, chopped
2 tbsp chopped fresh dill
6 canned anchovy fillets
    in oil, drained and
    chopped
5 hard-boiled eggs,
    roughly chopped
grated rind and juice of
    1 large lemon
365 g/12½ oz packet
    puff pastry
1 egg, beaten, for glaze
salt and pepper
lemon wedges and dill
    sprigs, to garnish

❶ Melt half of the butter in a large saucepan, add half the onion and cook for about 2 minutes, or until soft. Stir in the rice for 2 minutes, or until well coated.

❷ If necessary, add water to the reserved fish cooking liquid to make up to 225 ml/8 fl oz. Add to the rice, bring to the boil, then cover and cook very gently for about 18 minutes. Leave to cool.

❸ Melt the remaining butter in a frying pan, add the remaining onions and mushrooms, and cook for 8 minutes, or until there is no liquid. Add the spinach and dill. Season well, then cool.

❹ Add the anchovies, eggs, and lemon rind and juice to the mushroom mixture and toss well.

❺ Roll out the puff pastry and cut into two squares, one 28 cm/ 11 inches square and one 30 cm/12 inches square. Place the smaller piece on a greased baking sheet and spread half the mushroom mixture over, leaving a 2.5 cm/1 inch border; spoon half the rice over.

❻ Centre the salmon on top of the rice layer and cover with the remaining rice. Spoon the remaining mushroom mixture over. Drizzle the melted butter over the top. Brush the pastry edges with egg, cover with the second square and seal the edges.

❼ Brush with egg and mark a lattice pattern on top. Bake in a preheated oven 220°C/425°F/Gas Mark 7 for about 35 minutes, or until golden. Rest on a wire rack, then serve garnished.

❺

❻

easy

serves 4

25 minutes

1 hour, 5 minutes

Creole Jambalaya

INGREDIENTS

2 tbsp vegetable oil
85 g/3 oz piece smoked
    ham, cut into pieces
115 g/4 oz smoked pork
    sausage, cut in chunks
2 large onions, chopped
3 celery sticks, chopped
2 green peppers,
    deseeded, chopped
2 garlic cloves, chopped
225 g/8 oz chicken
    meat, cut into pieces
4 ripe tomatoes, peeled
    and chopped
175 ml/6 fl oz tomato
    sauce
450 ml/16 fl oz fish stock
400 g/14 oz long-grain
    white rice
4 spring onions, cut into
    2.5 cm/1 inch pieces
250 g/9 oz peeled raw
    prawns, tails on
250 g/9 oz cooked white
    crab meat
12 oysters, shelled

SEASONING MIX
2 dried bay leaves
2 tsp cayenne pepper
1½ tsp dried oregano
1 tsp ground white
    pepper, or to taste
salt and pepper

 very easy

 serves 4

 25 minutes

 45 minutes

❶ To make the seasoning mix, mix the ingredients in a bowl.

❷ Heat the oil in a flameproof casserole over medium heat. Add the smoked ham and the sausage and cook for about 8 minutes, stirring frequently, until golden. Using a slotted spoon, transfer to a large plate.

❸ Add the onions, celery and peppers to the casserole and cook for about 4 minutes, or until just softened. Stir in the garlic, then remove and set aside.

❹ Add the chicken pieces to the casserole and cook for 3–4 minutes, or until beginning to colour. Stir in the seasoning mix to coat.

❺ Return the ham, sausage and vegetables to the casserole and stir to combine. Add the chopped tomatoes and tomato sauce, then pour in the stock. Bring to the boil.

❻ Stir in the rice and reduce the heat to a simmer. Cook for about 12 minutes. Uncover, stir in the spring onions and prawns and cook, covered, for 4 minutes.

❼ Add the crab meat and oysters with their liquor and gently stir in. Cook until the rice is just tender, and the oysters slightly firm. Remove from the heat and leave to stand, covered, for about 3 minutes before serving.

Spicy Grilled Salmon

INGREDIENTS

4 salmon steaks, about
    175–225 g/6–8 oz each
lime slices, to garnish

MARINADE
4 garlic cloves, finely
    chopped
2 tbsp extra-virgin olive
    oil
pinch of ground allspice
pinch of ground
    cinnamon
juice of 2 limes
1–2 tsp marinade from
    canned chipotle
    chillies or bottled
    chipotle chilli salsa
¼ tsp ground cumin
pinch of sugar
salt and pepper

TO SERVE
tomato wedges
3 spring onions, finely
    chopped
shredded lettuce

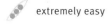 extremely easy

 serves 4

 5–10 minutes,
plus 1 hour to
marinate

6–8 minutes

❶ To make the marinade, finely chop the garlic and place in a bowl with the olive oil, allspice, cinnamon, lime juice, chipotle marinade, cumin and sugar. Add salt and pepper and stir to combine.

❷ Coat the salmon with the garlic mixture, then place in a non-metallic dish. Leave to marinate for at least an hour or overnight in the refrigerator.

❸ Transfer to a grill pan and cook under a preheated grill for 3–4 minutes on each side. Alternatively, cook the salmon over hot coals on a grill until cooked through.

❹ To serve, mix the tomato wedges with the spring onions. Place the salmon on individual plates and arrange the tomato salad and shredded lettuce alongside. Garnish with lime slices and serve.

COOK'S TIP
The marinade
also goes well with
fresh tuna steaks.

Fish Baked with Limes

 extremely easy

 serves 4

 10 minutes

 25 minutes

❶ Place the fish fillets in a bowl and sprinkle with salt and pepper. Squeeze the juice from the lime over the fish.

❷ Heat the olive oil in a frying pan. Add the onion and garlic and cook for about 2 minutes, stirring frequently, until softened. Remove from the heat.

❸ Place a third of the onion mixture and a little of the chillies and coriander in the bottom of a shallow baking dish or roasting tin. Arrange the fish on top. Top with the remaining onion mixture, chillies and coriander.

❹ Bake in a preheated oven at 180°C/350°F/Gas Mark 5 for 15–20 minutes, or until the fish has become slightly opaque and firm to the touch. Serve at once, with lemon and lime wedges for squeezing over the fish.

COOK'S TIP
Pickled jalapeños are called jalapeños en escabeche and are available from delicatessens.

VARIATION
Add canned chopped tomatoes to the mixture at the end of Step 2.

Baked Fish with Pepper, Chillies & Basil

INGREDIENTS

handful of fresh sweet
  basil leaves
750 g/1 lb 10 oz whole
  red snapper, sea bass
  or John Dory, cleaned
2 tbsp groundnut oil
2 tbsp Thai fish sauce
2 garlic cloves, crushed
1 tsp finely grated
  galangal or ginger
2 large fresh red chillies,
  sliced diagonally
1 yellow pepper,
  deseeded and diced
1 tbsp palm sugar (or
  brown sugar)
1 tbsp rice vinegar
2 tbsp water or fish
  stock
2 tomatoes, deseeded
  and sliced into thin
  wedges

❶ Reserve a few fresh basil leaves for garnish and tuck the rest inside the body cavity of the fish.

❷ Heat 1 tablespoon of oil in a wide frying pan and cook the fish quickly to brown, turning once. Place the fish on a large piece of foil in a roasting tin and spoon over the fish sauce. Wrap the foil over loosely and bake in an oven preheated to 190°C/375°F/ Gas Mark 5 for 25–30 minutes, or until just cooked though.

❸ Meanwhile, heat the remaining oil and cook the garlic, galangal and chilli for 30 seconds. Add the peppers and stir-fry for a further 2–3 minutes to soften.

❹ Stir in the sugar, rice vinegar and water, then add the tomatoe and bring to the boil. Remove the pan from the heat.

❺ Remove the fish from the oven and transfer to a warmed serving plate. Add the fish juices to the pan, then spoon the sauce over the fish and scatter with the reserved basil leaves. Serve immediately.

 extremely easy

 serves 4

 10 minutes

 35 minutes

❶  **❷**  **❸**

COOK'S TIP

Large red chillies are less hot than the tiny bird's eye chillies, so you can use them for a mild heat.

Spiced Tuna in Sweet-and-sour Sauce

INGREDIENTS

4 fresh tuna steaks,
    about 500 g/1 lb 2 oz
    total weight
¼ tsp ground black
    pepper
2 tbsp groundnut oil
1 onion, diced
1 small red pepper,
    deseeded and cut
    into matchsticks
1 garlic clove, crushed
½ cucumber, deseeded
    and cut into
    matchsticks
2 pineapple slices,
    diced
1 tsp finely chopped
    fresh ginger
1 tbsp soft light brown
    sugar
1 tbsp cornflour
1½ tbsp lime juice
1 tbsp Thai fish sauce
250 ml/8 fl oz fish stock

TO GARNISH
lime wedges
cucumber slices

❶ Sprinkle the tuna steaks with pepper on both sides. Heat a griddle or heavy frying pan and brush with a little of the oil. Arrange the tuna on the griddle and cook for about 8 minutes, turning them over once.

❷ Meanwhile, heat the remaining oil in another frying pan and cook the onion, pepper and garlic gently for 3–4 minutes to soften.

❸ Remove from the heat and stir in the cucumber, pineapple, ginger and sugar.

❹ Blend the cornflour with the lime juice and fish sauce, then stir into the stock and add to the frying pan. Stir over a medium heat until boiling, then cook for 1–2 minutes, or until thickened and clear.

❺ Spoon the sauce over the tuna and serve garnished with lime wedges and cucumber.

 extremely easy

 serves 4

 15 minutes

 8 minutes

Stir-fried Squid with Hot Black Bean Sauce

INGREDIENTS

750 g/1 lb 10 oz squid, cleaned
1 large red pepper, deseeded
100 g/3½ oz mangetouts, topped and tailed
1 head pak choi
3 tbsp black bean sauce
1 tbsp Thai fish sauce
1 tbsp rice wine
1 tbsp dark soy sauce
1 tsp soft light brown sugar
1 tsp cornflour
1 tbsp water
1 tbsp sunflower oil
1 tsp sesame oil
1 small red bird's eye chilli, chopped
1 garlic clove, finely chopped
1 tsp grated fresh ginger
2 spring onions, chopped

❶ Cut the tentacles from the squid and discard. Cut the body cavities into quarters lengthways. Use the tip of a small sharp knife to score a diamond pattern into the flesh, without cutting all the way through. Pat dry with kitchen paper.

❷ Cut the pepper into long, thin slices. Cut the mangetouts in half diagonally. Roughly shred the pak choi.

❸ Mix together the black bean sauce, fish sauce, rice wine, soy sauce and sugar. Blend the cornflour with the water and stir into the other ingredients. Keep to one side.

❹ Heat the oils in a wok. Add the chilli, garlic, ginger and spring onions and stir-fry for about 1 minute. Add the pepper and stir-fry for about 2 minutes.

❺ Add the squid and stir-fry over a high heat for a further minute. Stir in the mangetouts and pak choi and stir for a further minute, or until wilted.

❻ Stir in the sauce ingredients and cook, stirring, for 2 minutes, or until the sauce clears and thickens. Serve immediately.

 easy

 serves 4

 20 minutes

 10 minutes

Mackerel Escabeche

❶ Heat half the oil in a frying pan and dust the mackerel fillets with the seasoned flour.

❷ Add the fish to the frying pan and cook for about 30 seconds each side, or until not quite cooked through.

❸ Transfer the mackerel to a shallow dish, large enough to hold the fillets in one layer.

❹ Add the vinegar, onion, orange rind, thyme, rosemary, bay leaf garlic, chillies and salt to the frying pan. Simmer for 10 minutes.

❺ Add the remaining olive oil and the chopped parsley. Pour the mixture over the fish and leave until cold. Serve with plenty of crusty bread.

 extremely easy

 serves 4

5 minutes

12–15 minutes

Lemon Sole in a Sweet-and-sour Sauce

INGREDIENTS

2 large lemon sole,
   filleted
flour, to dredge
olive oil, to deep-fry
   plus 2 tbsp olive oil
2 onions, sliced thinly
150 g/5½ oz hazelnuts,
   chopped
75 g/2¾ oz pine kernels
40 g/1½ oz raisins
225 g/8 oz ripe
   tomatoes, skinned
   and chopped
2 tbsp red wine vinegar
125 ml/4 fl oz water
3 tbsp chopped fresh
   parsley
salt and pepper
boiled new potatoes,
   to serve

 very easy

 serves 4

 10 minutes

 1 hour

❶ Wash and dry the fish fillets. Dredge lightly with flour. In a large frying pan, heat about 2.5 cm/1 inch of olive oil — enough to just cover the fish — over medium-high heat. Add the fish fillets, 2 at a time, and completely submerge in the oil. Cook for 5–6 minutes, then drain on kitchen paper. Set aside. Cook the remaining fish the same way.

❷ Heat the remaining 2 tablespoons of olive oil in a large saucepan. Add the onions and cook for 7–8 minutes, or until soft and starting to brown. Add the hazelnuts, pine kernels and raisins and fry for a further 1–2 minutes, or until the nuts are golden. Add the tomatoes and cook for 5 minutes, or until softened.

❸ Add the vinegar and simmer for 5 minutes. Add the water, parsley and seasoning and stir well. Simmer for a further 5 minutes.

❹ Lower the fried fish into the sauce and simmer gently for 10 minutes. Serve with boiled new potatoes.

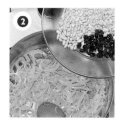

COOK'S TIP

In the Middle East, many different types of fish are treated this way, but a particular favourite is red mullet.

Cod Italienne

INGREDIENTS

2 tbsp olive oil
1 onion, finely chopped
2 garlic clove, finely
    chopped
2 tsp freshly chopped
    thyme
150 ml/5 fl oz red wine
400 g/14 oz canned
    chopped tomatoes
pinch sugar
40 g/1½ oz stoned black
    olives, roughly
    chopped
40 g/1½ oz stoned green
    olives, roughly
    chopped
2 tbsp capers, drained,
    rinsed and roughly
    chopped
2 tbsp chopped fresh
    basil
4 cod steaks, each
    weighing about
    175 g/6 oz
150 g/5½ oz ball buffalo
    mozzarella, drained
    and sliced
salt and pepper
buttered noodles,
    to serve

❶ Heat the olive oil in a large saucepan. Add the onion and cook gently for 5 minutes, or until softened but not coloured. Add the garlic and thyme and cook for a further minute.

❷ Add the red wine and increase the heat. Simmer until reduced and syrupy. Add the tomatoes and sugar and bring to the boil. Cover and simmer for 30 minutes. Uncover and simmer for a further 20 minutes, or until thick. Stir in the olives, capers and basil. Season to taste.

❸ Arrange the cod steaks in a shallow ovenproof dish (a lasagne dish is perfect) and spoon the tomato sauce over the top. Bake in a preheated oven at 190°C/375°F/Gas Mark 5 for 20–25 minutes, or until the fish is just tender.

❹ Remove from the oven and arrange the mozzarella slices on top of the fish.

❺ Return to the oven for a further 5–10 minutes, or until the cheese has melted. Serve immediately with buttered noodles.

 very easy

 serves 4

 10–15 minutes

 1 hour, 10
minutes

Home-salted Cod with Chickpeas

INGREDIENTS

1.5 kg/3 lb 5oz fresh
   boneless cod fillet,
   from the head end,
   skin on
225 g/8 oz dried chick-
   peas, soaked
   overnight
1 fresh red chilli
4 garlic cloves
2 bay leaves
1 tbsp olive oil
300 ml/10 fl oz chicken
   stock
pepper
extra-virgin olive oil,
to drizzle

GREMOLATA
3 tbsp chopped fresh
   parsley
2 garlic cloves, finely
   chopped
finely grated rind of
   1 lemon

❶ Sprinkle the salt over both sides of the cod fillet. Place in a shallow dish, cover and refrigerate for 48 hours. When ready to cook, remove the cod from the refrigerator and rinse under cold water. Leave to soak in cold water for 2 hours.

❷ Drain the chickpeas, rinse them thoroughly and drain again. Put into a large saucepan. Add double their volume of water and bring slowly to the boil. Skim the surface. Split the chilli lengthways and add to the chickpeas with the whole garlic cloves and bay leaves. Cover and simmer for 1½–2 hours, or until very tender, skimming occasionally if necessary.

❸ Drain the cod and pat dry. Brush with the olive oil and season well with black pepper (but no salt). Cook under a preheated grill or on a hot, ridged griddle for 3–4 minutes on each side, or until tender. Meanwhile, add the chicken stock to the chickpeas and bring back to the boil. Keep warm.

❹ For the gremolata, mix together the parsley, garlic and finely grated lemon rind.

❺ To serve, ladle the chickpeas and their cooking liquid into 6 warmed soup bowls. Top with the grilled cod and sprinkle over the gremolata. Drizzle generously with olive oil and serve.

 easy

 serves 4

 5 minutes,
   plus 50 hours to
   salt, then soak

 2½ hours

Moroccan Fish Tagine

INGREDIENTS

2 tbsp olive oil
1 large onion, finely
    chopped
large pinch saffron
    strands
½ tsp ground cinnamon
1 tsp ground coriander
½ tsp ground cumin
½ tsp ground turmeric
200 g/7 oz canned
    chopped tomatoes
300 ml/10 fl oz fish stock
4 small red mullet
    cleaned, boned and
    heads and tails
    removed
85 g/3 oz stoned green
    olives
1 tbsp chopped
    preserved lemon
3 tbsp fresh chopped
    coriander
salt and pepper
couscous, to serve

❶ Heat the olive oil in a large saucepan or flameproof casserole. Add the onion and cook gently for 10 minutes without colouring until softened. Add the saffron, cinnamon, coriander, cumin and turmeric and cook for a further 30 seconds, stirring.

❷ Add the chopped tomatoes and fish stock and stir well. Bring to the boil, cover and simmer for 15 minutes. Uncover and simmer for a further 20–35 minutes, or until thickened.

❸ Cut each red mullet in half, then add the pieces to the pan, pushing them into the sauce. Simmer gently for a further 5–6 minutes, or until the fish is just cooked.

❹ Carefully stir in the olives, preserved lemon and the chopped coriander. Season to taste and serve with couscous.

 extremely easy

 serves 4

 10 minutes

 50 minutes

Smoked Fish Pie

INGREDIENTS

2 tbsp olive oil
1 onion, finely chopped
1 leek, thinly sliced
1 carrot, diced
1 celery stick, diced
115 g/4 oz button
   mushrooms
grated rind 1 lemon
350 g/12 oz skinless,
   boneless smoked cod
   or haddock fillet, cubed
350 g/12 oz skinless,
   boneless white fish,
   cubed
225 g/8 oz cooked
   peeled prawns
2 tbsp chopped parsley
1 tbsp chopped fresh dill

SAUCE
55 g/2 oz butter
50 g/1¾ oz plain flour
1 tsp mustard powder
600 ml/1 pint milk
55 g/2 oz Gruyère
   cheese, grated

TOPPING
675 g/1½ lb potatoes
55 g/2 oz butter, melted
25 g/1 oz Gruyère
   cheese, grated
salt and pepper

❶ For the sauce, melt the butter in a saucepan and add the flour and mustard powder. Stir until smooth and cook over a low heat for 2 minutes without colouring. Beat in the milk. Simmer for 2 minutes, then stir in the cheese until smooth. Remove from the heat and put clingfilm over the surface to prevent a skin forming. Set aside.

❷ For the topping, boil the whole potatoes in salted water for 15 minutes. Drain well and set aside until cool enough to handle.

❸ Heat the oil in a clean pan and add the onion. Cook until softened. Halve the button mushroomns and add them with the leek, carrot and celery, and cook for 10 minutes more, or until the vegetables have softened. Stir in the lemon rind and cook briefly.

❹ Add the softened vegetables with the fish, prawns, parsley, and dill to the sauce. Season, then transfer to a greased casserole dish.

❺ Peel the potatoes and grate roughly. Mix with the melted butter. Cover the filling with the potato and sprinkle with the grated cheese.

❻ Cover with foil and bake in a preheated oven at 200°C/400°F/ Gas Mark 6 for 30 minutes. Remove the foil and bake for a further 30 minutes, or until the topping is golden and the filling bubbling Serve immediately with a selection of your favourite vegetables.

 easy

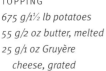 serves 4

 35–40 minutes

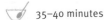 1 hour,
20 minutes